# Touring the W
# and the Western Isles of
# Scotland

A guide to help you plan the trip of a
lifetime

by
Paul Bissett

For all the wonderful friendly people, we met touring this area.

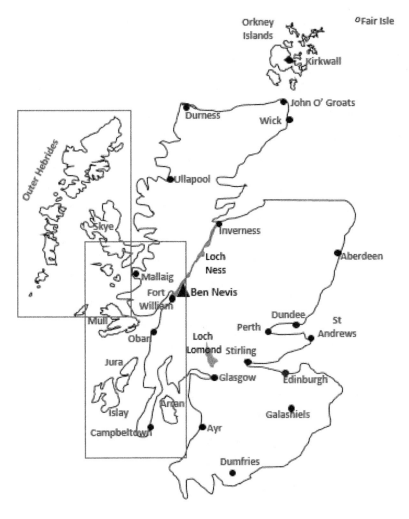

Map of Scotland

# Table of Contents

# Chapter 1

## Plan Your Trip

Having traveled to over forty countries and lived in seven, I have learned a thing or two about traveling, mainly through making mistakes, for instance;

We caught a ferry to France but didn't bother changing money prior to boarding. Again, we could have changed our money on the ferry but didn't. We thought (wrongly)we could change our pounds to francs when we got to France. When we arrived, my friends and I spent the day trying to get our money changed, with no luck, we spent the last few hours of our day trip in a bar at the ferry terminal that would accept British pounds. Lesson learned -- always change enough money to last a few days prior to leaving (not as important in this day of credit cards, but better safe than sorry).

You can change your money at the airport when you get there, after checking your bags and going through security (if the money exchange is open) or we have recently found it's fairly easy to find ATM's to take out local currencies from your local bank. It is still possible to order foreign currency from your bank before you leave (for a small fee, of course). It's also a very good idea to let your bank and credit card companies know the dates and destinations of your travel, so you don't have declined payments.

On another trip, my wife and I decided to tour around Europe and not book any accommodation in advance. Our plan (if you can call it that) was that if we liked a place, we would stay an extra day, if not we would move on. We flew into Frankfurt (when the Book Fair was on) and struggled to get a hotel. Where we stayed was less than ideal (to say the least). Next day we drove down to Munich for Octoberfest, knowing Munich would be booked out, we stopped in Augsburg about 50 miles north and tried to get a room. They told us the whole town was sold out for Octoberfest and the European Rodeo Finals (honest). We found a room at a farmhouse after hours of looking. After Octoberfest, we drove down South and tried to get a room in Oberammergau -- guess what? Their world renowned "Passion Play," which they put on once every ten years, was on that weekend; no hotels to be had.

A few days later we arrived in Paris at the same time as the European Auto Show was on – again, hotels booked out. It was the same when we got to Amsterdam. That trip makes for a funny story, over a few drinks, but was actually very stressful. So, book your rooms in advance; for some areas with limited accommodation, book as much as a year in advance, but also call up and confirm your booking with six months to go and again with three months to go.

We had a hotel in Scotland that changed ownership and lost our booking, fortunately we caught it at the six-month point.

On a different trip to Paris, apart from the obvious sites, we also wanted to see Rodin's Garden. Although we kept an eye open for it as we visited everything else, we never saw it. Each time we left the hotel we turned right, when the taxi picked us up to take us to the airport, it went left. Guess what was just around the corner; yes, it was Rodin's Garden.

It was at that point I decided to plan all future trips like they were a military campaign. When going on vacation, be it to a foreign country or a road trip, we discuss what we want to see and book our hotels based on that. I then research as much as possible, as to what there is to see and do in that area, also where to eat. This can mean that there are more things to see than time to see them. So, while there, we decide what we are going to see and what we're going to skip, based on how tired we are or what we have seen already. At least this way the choice is ours and we didn't miss something, that was just around the corner.

Something to consider when going to Scotland (well, the entirety of the UK) is driving. They drive on the left side of the road and their road signs and markings are usually different. If you drive an automatic at home, then be sure to book one in Scotland. I got a manual drive car in London and stalled it five times in the parking area before going back into the rental office and getting an automatic. If you are going rural in Scotland, the roads can be very narrow. So be aware that the bigger the car you get, the less room there is for other cars/trucks to get past you (and you them) on those narrow roads and it can be scary. We base the car size on the amount of luggage we have.

Do you even need a car?  If you are staying in a city or large town there are buses/trams/taxis/trains to be had.  We like to go all over Scotland, so usually do rent a car, but when we get back to Edinburgh (that's where we usually fly in and out from), we return the car to the rental office and take our luggage into town either by taxi or tram for the last few days of our vacation, as we don't need a car in Edinburgh and the traffic (and parking)can be really bad.

You can also stay in a town close by that has direct bus and train links, such as Linlithgow or Stirling.

## Planning

You know you want to go to Scotland, but when exactly, and what do you want to see/do? Ideally, you will be thinking at least a year ahead.  Can you book it in less time?  Of course, you can, but if you are going into more rural areas, such as the Highlands, there are fewer accommodation options and they book out fast.

First, do a little research and make a list of what you want to see and do.  This should also help you work out when you want to go, if for instance you want to go for Hogmanay (New Year) in Edinburgh, you will have to go in late December.  If you wish to Visit the Edinburgh Festival, you go in August.

If you have no such date/time restraints, think about:

- The weather (historically, April and September have the least rain).

- Whatever time of year take a coat, it will likely rain at some point.

- Think about attractions being open (some close during the winter).

- Think about midges (See Additional Information in Chapter 6).

OK, you have your list and your dates. What I do now is look on Google maps to see where my priorities are geographically. This allows me to pick a start and finish point and overnight stays in between.
I now have a rough guide to my trip, but I don't book anything yet.
I continue working on Google maps and type in (for example) hotels in Fort William. This shows all the hotels and their prices. I can now pick a hotel location that works for us, usually based on walking distance to bars/restaurants, unless it is a destination hotel with everything we could need on premises.
I don't base the hotel selection on how close it is to something we want to visit (within reason), as we have the car, if that's how we're getting around(this is our preferred option as it is more flexible than public transport).
I now take the hotel information and research it online, Hotels.com, Kayak, Trip Advisor, Expedia etc., I find the best deal and make a note of it. We have found, through frustrating experience, that booking through one of these sites CAN greatly reduce any flexibility that might be needed. I prefer to book flights and hotels through their own websites as much as possible. You might need to get home sooner than expected or might even want to extend your trip – some of these travel websites are a

nightmare to get ahold of and/or won't let you change your itinerary.

Now it's time to work out how long it will take to get to our hotel via the things we want to see and do;

how long it takes by car to our first stop.

I then allocate an approximate amount of time at our first stop, depending on what it is, then work out how long to our next stop and so forth.

This gives me a rough idea of how long a day it will be, and we can adjust as necessary.  This may appear to be overkill, but it really does help to know what time you should set off and what time you can expect to arrive at your destination.

## Here is an example day from our last trip;

**Sat - Sep 29th** (8.5 hours)

- Set off at 8:30am - 1.5 hour to Glamis Castle (opens at 10am - allow 2 hours to tour castle)

- 1 hour to the old course at St. Andrews for lunch (allow 1hour)

- 1.5 hours' drive to Dunnotter Castle (allow 1 hour to tour castle)

- 45 minutes to our hotel, McLeod Lodge (dinner booked)

Does it always work out the way I planned?
Not always. For instance, we ended up having a light lunch in the kitchen cafe at Glamis Castle and didn't go to St. Andrews for lunch.  We also stopped in

Stonehaven after Dunnotter Castle, before carrying on to our hotel, but we made those informed choices because we knew our time constraints and what there was to see enroute.

What type of clothes should you take? Well, that will mainly be down to the time of year you choose to go. Choose layers so you can add or take off clothes as needed. No matter what time of year we go, we always take a rainproof coat or jacket. One trip, my wife, Tracey, forgot (wink-wink) a raincoat, so we stopped by a thrift store and she found one she liked for very little money. Comfortable shoes/boots are always a good idea. There are a lot of castles and other outdoor sites that need good footwear. I always take a baseball cap as it can keep the sun and rain out of your eyes. Other than that, just clothes that you are comfortable in, and something a bit dressier if you are planning a night out or a nice dinner.

The thing to remember is, you will have your suitcases with you in the car most of the time. You can almost always access extra clothing (if you have it with you). Also, if you need to, you can always buy something there.

## Something to consider

Should you buy a pass or membership that gets you discounts to castles, stately homes or a city pass? We did a few years ago but were disappointed to find that many of the sites we visited were not members, so had to pay anyway.

My suggestion is, if you are considering it, make a list of which sites you want to visit and check that against what the pass gets you into, if it's a match, go ahead it will save you money.

But be aware that some passes are time sensitive, such as the "Edinburgh City Pass." This pass will save you 25% on normal entrance fees, but is only good for 48 hours, so you had better be committed to getting around the attractions.

# Eating out

From food trucks to Michelin Starred restaurants, you are spoiled for choice. Scotland has great locally sourced food, from its abundant seafood, game, Black Angus (Aberdeen Angus) beef, and lamb, to its fruits and berries. You can pair great meals with any number of whiskies or gins, fine local ales and imported wines (we don't have the weather for grapes).

Suffice it to say that we have eaten in fish-n-chip shops, bars, pubs, diners, and Michelin Starred restaurants. We haven't had a bad meal and have had some memorable ones.

Be brave and try some of the local dishes like haggis (Scotland is the only place where it is made properly due to other countries' restrictions on the contents). On our last trip we both had haggis on the first four days. Dishes such as Cullen Skink (fish soup), tattie scones, (potato scones), cranachan(dessert), scotch pies, black pudding, red pudding, white pudding (savories, not "pudding" in any American sense), stovies (variation on corned beef hash) and Arbroath Smokies (smoked fish) should be given a try.

# Hotels

I was born and raised in Scotland and most of my family still live there. On several occasions we have stayed with family and used their house (or holiday home) as a base for our trips. Where we have stayed in a hotel, I have mentioned it. We have been happy with all our accommodations in Scotland, comparing what we paid for it, against the quality of the room and the service we received.

Please remember that hotel ownership may change, so your stay may differ from ours. Just because we liked it, does not guarantee that you will.

The one thing I will not do, is book a room in a hotel that does not have a website. Does that guarantee everything will be perfect? No, it doesn't, but I like to get an idea of what the hotel looks like and what is on offer there. So far, it has worked out for us.

# Populations

I have given populations (approx.) of towns as a rough guide to what you may expect as far as amenities that may be available by the size of the population.

# Maps

The map at the start of each chapter shows the area that is covered in that chapter.  This is a general guide and I recommend that you get a proper map to plan your trip with and take it with you.  Being from Scotland, I was taking my American wife around and she asked for a map so she could get a better perspective of where things were.  We bought a Collins Road Map Scotland.

# GPS

I'm now going to state the obvious, if you are using a GPS, be aware that it will take you the most direct route.  For instance, if you are starting the day in Ullapool and intend to finish the day at Wick, it will take you by the shortest route across country and you will miss about half of the NC500.
Look at the map and use your GPS for waypoints such as Durness, then John O' Groats etc.

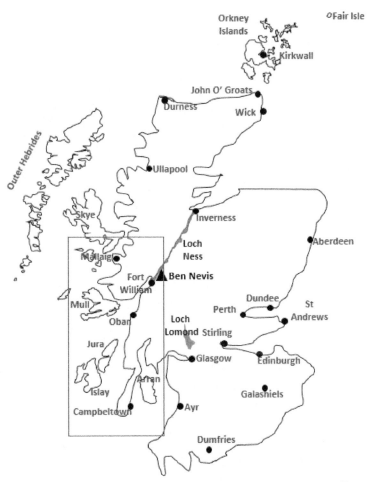

Arran, Campbeltown, Oban, Isla, Jura, Mull, Fort
William and Mallaig.

# Chapter 2

## Kintyre and the West

### The Isle of Arran

Often referred to as Scotland in miniature (20 miles north-south and 10 miles east-west), with mountains, glens, lochs, beaches and whisky. If you are bringing over a car, it's wise to fill your tank before you come. Gas (petrol) can be expensive on the isle and there are not that many Gas (petrol) stations. I am using Brodick as the start and finish point with distances from there, on a circular trip around the island (Counter-clockwise).

### Getting there, by Ferry (the only option)

- From Ardrossan, Mainland to Brodick, Arran.

- From Campbeltown, Kintyre to Brodick, Arran.

- From Claonaig, Kintyre to Lochranza, Arran **Summer only.**

- From Tarbert, Kintyre to Lochranza, Arran **Winter only.**
  www.calmac.co.uk

# Brodick (Pop. 600)

The main port and second biggest town.

- Hotels, B&Bs, Food, Drink, Car Hire, Buses, Taxis, Shops, ATMs/Banks, **Gas (petrol) & Charging Stations**.

## Brodick Highland Games

- Held in Early-August each year. Tossing the Caber, Highland dancing, Athletics, and Pipe bands.
  www.facebook.com/BrodickHighlandGames
  *Ormidale Park, Brodick.*

## Heritage Museum

- History, archaeology and geology of the isle.
  www.arranmuseum.co.uk
  *Brodick.*

## Arran Brewery (2 miles from Brodick)

- Tours and tastings. See website for details.
  www.arranbrewery.co.uk

## Brodick Castle (3 miles from Brodick)

- There has been a castle on this site for centuries, but the present building dates from 1844. www.nts.org.uk/visit/places/brodick-castle-garden-country-park

## Isle of Arran Distillery (14 miles from Brodick)

- Pronunciation:  Ar-ran.

- Name Origin:  Named for the island on which it is located.

- Established:  1995.

- Location:  Lochranza, Isle of Arran.

- Region:  Island.

- Visitor Center/Tours:  Go to website for information.

- Website: www.arranwhisky.com

## Lochranza Castle (14 miles from Brodick)

- Only a shell of the castle now remains, open to people and sheep.

## The Sailor's Grave (15 miles from Brodick)

- In 1854 a sailor by the name of John McLean had died onboard ship and the crew wanted him buried in Lochranza, but the people were fearful that he may have had the plague, so refused.
  So, he was buried by the roadside outside of the village. It has become a custom to add a pebble to his grave if you stop there.

## Auchagallon Stone Circle (9 miles from Brodick)

- A cross between a Cairn and a stone circle. This might be a good point to finish your day and head back to Brodick, if you are staying there, as you will have finished the top half of the island.

## Kings Cave (11 miles from Brodick)

- Short walk from the parking area, sensible footwear recommended.
  https://forestryandland.gov.scot/visit/kings-cave

## Machrie Moor Standing Stones (12 miles from Brodick)

- Can be a bit boggy under foot, so consider your footwear.

## Blackwaterfoot (14 miles from Brodick)

- Hotels, B&Bs, Food, Drink, Buses, Taxis, Shops, ATM, **Gas (petrol)**.

## Glenashdale Falls & Giants Graves (9 miles from Brodick)

- 3 miles circular walk to see the falls and the Giants graves (2 Neolithic chambered tombs).

# Lamlash (Pop. 1,000)

The biggest town on the isle.

- Hotels, B&Bs, Food, Drink, Buses, Taxis, Shops, ATM, **Gas (petrol) & Charging Stations**.

# Arran Coastal Way

- A hiking circuit around the isle of Arran.
  Distance: 66mi/109km
  Duration: 10 days
  Height Gain:  6863ft/2092m*
  *This is dependent on whether you take in
  Goatfell mountain or any of the alternate
  routes or not.
  www.coastalway.co.uk

# Campbeltown (Pop. 4,800)

I am now using Campbeltown as the start point, with distances from there. We spent six days in Campbeltown while I was doing the Whisky School at the Springbank Distillery. As you head North, your options as to which direction to travel really open up; out to Islay, Jura, Mull and Iona or carry on up the West coast, turn off to the Cowal Peninsula or head into the mainland. From Campbeltown the route I have followed will take you to Oban, Fort William and finally Mallaig, with alternate routes shown, but always coming back to the North.

## Getting there, Campbeltown Airport;

- From Glasgow
  www.hial.co.uk/campbeltown-airport

## By Bus

- Citylink
  www.citylink.co.uk

## By Ferry

- To/From Ardrossan.

- To/From Brodick, Arran.
  www.calmac.co.uk

## Kintyre Express (boat)

- To/From Ballycastle, Northern Ireland.

- To/From Port Ellen, Islay.
  https://kintyreexpress.com

## Campbeltown

- Hotels, B&Bs, Food, Drink, shops, Buses, Taxis, Car Hire, ATMs/Banks, Hospital, Post Office, **Gas (petrol) & Charging Stations**. There a number of accommodations to be had in and around town, and out in the countryside. We stayed at the following hotel and would happily recommend it;

## Ardshiel Hotel

- The food was superb, the whisky selection huge (over 700), and the staff very friendly.
  https://ardshiel.co.uk
  *Kilkerran Road.*

## Campbeltown Heritage Center

- Over 300 years of history from Campbeltown and the Kintyre Peninsula.
  https://campbeltownheritagecentre.co.uk

## Campbeltown Malts Festival

- Held annually every May. A 3-day celebration of Glengyle, Glen Scotia and Springbank. Campbeltown's 3 whisky distilleries. www.explorecampbeltown.com

## Campbeltown Museum

- The story of Kintyre. www.argyll-bute.gov.uk

## Glen Gyle Distillery

- Pronunciation: Glen-Gile

- Name Origin: Gaelic - "Valley - Middle English *gyle*, from Middle Dutch *gijl*, to boil, ferment.

- Established: 2004.

- Location: Glengyle Road, Campbeltown.

- Region: Campbeltown.

- Visitor Center/Tours: Go to website for information.

- Website: https://kilkerran.scot

## Glen Scotia

- Pronunciation:  Glen-Scosha.

- Name Origin:  Gaelic - "Valley of the Scots."

- Established:  1832.

- Location:  12 High Street, Campbeltown.

- Region:  Campbeltown.

- Visitor Center/Tours:  Go to website for information.

- Website: www.glenscotia.com

## Linda McCartney Memorial Garden

- Quiet garden in the center of town dedicated to Paul McCartney's late wife.
www.lindasgarden.co.uk

## Mull of Kintyre Music Festival

- Held annually every August in Campbeltown.
www.explorecampbeltown.com

## Mull of Kintyre Sea Tours

- Powerboat "Seafaris."

## Springbank Distillery

- Pronunciation: Spring-Bank.

- Name Origin: Spring (water) from a bank.

- Established: 1828.

- Location: 9 Bolgam Street, Campbeltown.

- Region: Campbeltown.

- Visitor Center/Tours: Go to website for information.

- Website: http://springbank.scot

## Springbank Whisky School

- Five-day school with hands on whisky making. http://springbank.scot/whisky-school

## Davaar Island

- A tidal island reached by the *Dhorlin* shingle causeway at low tide. On the island is Stevenson lighthouse, and several caves with a painting of the crucifixion in one.

# Heading North from Campbeltown

## Sadell Abbey (10 miles from Campbeltown)

- Now a ruin, this Cistercian monastery was in use between 1207-1507.

## <u>Beinn An Tuirc</u> Distillery (13 miles from Campbeltown)

- Makers of Kintyre Gin.
  <u>www.kintyregin.com</u>
  *Lephincorrach Farmhouse Torrisdale Castle Estate*

## Kennacraig Ferry Terminal (32 miles from Campbeltown)

- There's not much here, but there is a **Charging Station.**

- For ferries to Islay.
  www.calmac.co.uk

# Side Trip East from Kennacraig

## Skipness Castle (8 miles East from Kennacraig Ferry)

- 13<sup>th</sup> century castle and Chapel.
  www.historicenvironment.scot/visit-a-place/places/skipness-castle-and-chapel

# We are about to take a detour to Islay from Kennacraig.

## To continue on the route North, see page 47.

# Isle of Islay (Pop. 3,200)
### (Pronounced Eye-la)

Across the sea to the West is Islay, known as the "Queen of the Hebrides," covering an area of 239 sq. miles, with nothing more than 18 miles from Bowmore, the capital. All distances will be shown from Bowmore. Islay is rightly famous for its whisky distilleries, details below. There is a wealth of accommodations to be had on Islay.

## Getting there, Islay Airport;

- From, Edinburgh and Glasgow.
  www.hial.co.uk/islay-airport

- From Oban, mainland.
  www.hebrideanair.co.uk

## By Ferry

- From Kennacraig, mainland to Port Ellen, Islay.

- From Kennacraig, mainland to Askaig, Islay.
  www.calmac.co.uk

## Kintyre Express Ferry

- To/From Ballycastle, Northern Ireland (foot traffic only) to Port Ellen, Islay.

- To/From Campbeltown (foot traffic only) to Port Ellen, Islay.
  https://kintyreexpress.com

## Cantilena Festival

- Chamber Music performed by Cantilena's professional musicians and students of the Royal Conservatoire of Scotland. Held annually in July at various venues on Islay.
  www.cantilenafestival.co.uk

## Feis Ile

- Islay Festival with; Ceilidhs, Gaelic lessons, Golf, Music, Poetry and Whisky. Held annually at various venues across the isle in late May. www.islayfestival.com

## Islay Jazz Festival

- Held annually in September at various venues on Islay. www.islayjazzfestival.co.uk

# Bowmore (Pop. 1000)

Famous for its whisky distillery (the 2$^{nd}$ oldest in Scotland). Next to the distillery is the MacTaggart Leisure Center whose swimming pool is warmed by Bowmore Distillery's surplus heat.

- Hotels, B&Bs, Food, Drink, Shops, Buses, ATMs/Banks, Post Office, **Gas (petrol) Station & Charging points.**

## Bowmore Distillery (2nd oldest in Scotland)

- Pronunciation:  Bo-more.

- Name Origin:  Gaelic - Big Hut."

- Established:  1779.

- Location:  School street, Bowmore.

- Region:  Islay.

- Visitor Center/Tours:  Go to website for information.

- Website: www.bowmore.com

## Islay Whisky Academy

- Tours & Education.
  www.islaywhiskyacademy.scot

## Kilarrow Church

- Known as the "Round Church" and built in 1769.
  www.undiscoveredscotland.co.uk/islay/roundc hurch/index.html

## Nerabus Gin Distillery (3 miles from Bowmore)

- Makers of Nerabus Islay dry gin.
  www.islayginltd.com


## Bruichladdich Distillery (9 miles from Bowmore)

- Pronunciation:  Brook-laddy.

- Name Origin:  Gaelic - "The Bank of the Shore."

- Established:  1881.

- Location:  Bruichladdich distillery, Islay.

- Region:  Islay.

- Visitor Center/Tours:  Go to website for information.

- Website: www.bruichladdich.com

*Bruichladdich and Kilchoman distilleries are close to each other.

## Finlaggan (10 miles from Bowmore)

- The ruin of the home of the "Lords of the Isles" and looked upon as the "Cradle of Clan Donald."
www.finlaggan.org

## Museum of Island Life (10 miles from Bowmore)

- With items from the Mesolithic period (10,000 years ago) to 1950.
www.islaymuseum.org

## Port Ellen Village (10 miles from Bowmore)

- Hotels, B&Bs, Food, Drink, Shops, Bicycle& Electric Bicycle hire, buses, ATMs/Banks, Post Office, **Gas (petrol) Station &Charging points.**

**Caol Ila** (11 miles from Bowmore)

- Pronunciation:  Cool-Eye-Lah.

- Name Origin:  Gaelic - "Sound of Islay."

- Established:  1846.

- Location:  Port Askaig, Islay.

- Region:  Islay.

- Visitor Center/Tours:  Go to website for information.

- Website:  www.malts.com/en-gb/visit-our-distilleries/caol-ila

*Caol Ila, Ardnahoe and Bunnahabhain Distilleries are close to each other.

**Islay Boat Trips** (Port Askaig,11 miles from Bowmore)

- A variety of tours available, with the trip to the whirlpool of Corryvreckan, the 3rd largest in the world a highlight. When the tide is right, its roar can be heard ten miles away. www.islayinfo.com/islay-boat-trips.html

## Ardnahoe Distillery (12 miles from Bowmore)

- Pronunciation:  Ard-na-ho.

- Name Origin:  "Height of the Hollow."

- Established:  2018.

- Location:  Near Port Askaig, Islay.

- Region:  Islay.

- Visitor Center/Tours:  Go to website for information.

- Website: https://ardnahoedistillery.com

## Kilchoman Distillery (12 miles from Bowmore)

- Pronunciation:  Kil-Ho-Man

- Name Origin:  Gaelic - "St Comman's church."

- Established:  2005.

- Location:  Rockside Farm, Bruichladdich.

- Region:  Islay.

- Visitor Center/Tours:  Go to website for information.

- Website: https://kilchomandistillery.com

**Laphroaig** (12 miles from Bowmore)

- Pronunciation: La-Froy-g.

- Name Origin: Gaelic - "Hollow by the big bay."

- Established: 1815.

- Location: Laphroaig, Islay.

- Region: Islay.

- Visitor Center/Tours: Go to website for information.

- Website: www.laphroaig.com

*Laphroaig, Lagavulin and Ardbeg are close to each other.

## **Bunnahabhain Distillery** (13 miles from Bowmore)

- Pronunciation:  Boo-na-Hav-ven.

- Name Origin:  Gaelic - "Foot (bottom) of the River."

- Established:  1883.

- Location:  Bunnahabhain, Islay.

- Region:  Islay.

- Visitor Center/Tours:  Go to website for information.

- Website: https://bunnahabhain.com

## Lagavulin (13 miles from Bowmore)

- Pronunciation: Lag-a-Voo-Lin.

- Name Origin: *Gaelic* - "Hollow of the Mill."

- Established: 1816.

- Location: Lagavulin, Islay.

- Region: Islay.

- Visitor Center/Tours: Go to website for information.

- Website: www.malts.com/en-gb/visit-our-distilleries/lagavulin

## Islay Sea Adventures (Lagavulin,13 miles from Bowmore)

- A variety of tours available, with the trip to the whirlpool of Corryvreckan, the 3$^{rd}$ largest in the world a highlight. When the tide is right, its roar can be heard ten miles away. www.islayinfo.com/islay-boat-trips.html

## Ardbeg (14 miles from Bowmore)

- Pronunciation:  Ard-beg.

- Name Origin:  Gaelic - "An Àird Bheag," meaning "The Small Promontory."

- Established:  1815.

- Location:  Port Ellen.

- Region:  Islay.

- Visitor Center/Tours:  Go to website for information.

- Website: www.ardbeg.com

## American Monument (15 miles from Bowmore)

- The monument was erected at the Oa (a rocky headland) in 1920 by The American Red Cross to commemorate the loss (close by) of American Sailors and Soldiers from two shipwrecks. www.lovefromscotland.co.uk/isle-of-islay-scotland

# Kildalton Cross (18 miles from Bowmore)

- The Kildalton Cross is still standing where it was first erected more than 1,200 years ago, making it one of very few early Christian Celtic crosses still in their original position. www.historicenvironment.scot/visit-a-place/places/kildalton-cross

# Isle of Jura (Pop. 200)

Just North of "Islay" is the Isle of "Jura," 30 miles long by 7 miles wide, with few people and around 7,000 Red Deer. Most visitors come here as part of a trip to nearby Islay. There is a bus service on Jura's one and only road, otherwise bring your own car or bicycle. Craighouse is the main village and has the only shop, hotel and pub on the island, the only two places to eat. Accommodation on Jura is limited, so if you wish to stay here, book early, your other option is to stay on Islay and come over on the ferry for a day trip. I am using the port of Feolin as the start point, with distances from there.

- Hotel, B&Bs, Self-Catering, Food, Drink, Shop, **Gas (petrol) Station.**

**By Ferry** (the only option, no need to book, pay onboard)

- From Askaig, Islay to Feolin, Jura. www.calmac.co.uk

# Jura Boat Tours

- A variety of tours available, with the trip to the whirlpool of Corryvreckan, the 3$^{rd}$ largest in the world a highlight. When the tide is right, its roar can be heard ten miles away. www.juraboattours.co.uk

# Jura Distillery (8 miles from Feolin)

- Pronunciation: Ju-Rah

- Name Origin: Old Norse - "Doirad's Island."

- Established: 1963.

- Location: Craighouse, Isle of Jura.

- Region: Island.

- Visitor Center/Tours: Go to website for information.

- Website: https://jurawhisky.com

## **Lussa Distillery** (25 miles from Feolin)

- Makers of Lussa Gin.
  www.lussagin.com

# Kennacraig & and the route North

## Tarbert (Pop. 1300)
### (5 miles North from Kennacraig Ferry)

My enduring memory of Tarbert, is from back in the late 70s. I was in the area with the Navy and was sitting in the "Frigate Bar" having a beer after hours. I looked to my left and there was a Police Sergeant, I thought we were all in trouble, but he took his hat off and ordered a whisky, fortunately he was off duty. I will now use Tarbert as the start point, with distances from there.

- Hotel, B&Bs, Self-Catering, Food, Drink, Shops, ATM/Bank, Buses, Medical Center, **Gas (petrol) & Charging Station.**
www.tarbertlochfyne.com

## Ferry Terminal (Tarbert)

- From/to Portavadie.
  www.calmac.co.uk

## Tarbert Castle Heritage Park

- The ruined structure of a medieval castle offers stunning views over the surrounding area. The Castle Heritage Park provides an excellent family picnic spot close to the village.

## Scottish Series Yacht Regatta

- The second biggest yachting event in Britain, with several hundred yachts participating. Held Annually in May.
  www.tarbertlochfyne.com

## Tarbert Music Festival

- Featuring contemporary and traditional Scottish Music. Held Annually in mid-September.
  www.tarbertlochfyne.com

## Tarbert Seafood Festival

- Held Annually in the first full weekend of July. www.tarbertlochfyne.com

## Stonefield Castle Hotel (2 miles from Tarbert)

- Scottish baronial styled castle dating back to 1837. www.bespokehotels.com/stonefieldcastle *Stonefield, Tarbert.*

# Ardrishaig Village
### (11 Miles from Tarbert)

- Hotel, B&Bs, Food, Drink, Shops, Post Office, ATM, Buses & Taxis.

## Kilberry Sculptured Stones (15 Miles West from Tarbert)

- A collection of ancient grave markers.

# Lochgilphead
### (14 Miles North from Tarbert)

I will now use Lochgilphead as the start point, with distances from there.

- Hotel, B&Bs, Food, Drink, Hospital& Medical Center, Shops, Post Office, ATMs/Banks, Buses & Taxis.

## From Lochgilphead you can head North/West or North/East

**For the route North and West to Oban, Fort William and Mallaig see page 59.**

# First the alternate route from Lochgilphead heading North/East, then South to the Isle of Bute.

**Crarae Garden** (14 Miles North from Lochgilphead)

- Waterfalls and Britain's finest example of a Himalayan-style garden. Visitor center, shop and café.
  www.nts.org.uk/visit/places/crarae-garden

**Auchindrain** (19 Miles North from Lochgilphead)

- A 22-acre museum, representing an important part of Scotland's past, showing how most people lived in Scotland prior to the 1700s. Containing the houses and other buildings of a small farming community known as a "**township**."
  www.auchindrain.org.uk

# Inveraray (Pop. 600)
## (25 Miles North East from Lochgilphead)

I will now use the town of Inveraray as the start point, with distances from there.

- Hotels, B&Bs, Food, Drink, Shops, ATM/Bank, Buses, **Gas (petrol) & Charging Station.**

## Inveraray Jail

- Tour an old prison built in 1820.
  www.inverarayjail.co.uk

## Inveraray Bell Tower

- Built to commemorate the members of Clan Campbell who died in the First World War. You can climb to the top for great views.
  www.inveraraybelltower.co.uk

## Inveraray Castle

- Iconic castle and ancestral home of the Duke of Argyll, Chief of the Clan Campbell.
  www.inveraray-castle.com

## Inveraray Highland Games

- Held in Mid-July each year. Tossing the Caber, Highland dancing, Athletics, and Pipe bands.
  http://inveraray-games.co.uk
  *Inveraray Castle.*

## Dun Na Cuaiche watchtower (1 mile walk from Inveraray castle)

- Or you can drive almost all the way up, either way it's worth the effort for the view.
  www.inveraray-castle.com/walking

# We now head around the top of Loch Fyne and down south to Dunoon and the Isle of Bute.

**Benmore Botanical gardens** (32 miles from Inveraray)

- 120-acre mountainside garden. www.rbge.org.uk/visit/benmore-botanic-garden

# Dunoon (Pop. 4500)
## (39 miles from Inveraray)

The main town on the Cowal Peninsula. There is a wealth of accommodations to be had in and around town.

- Hotels, B&Bs, Food, Drink, Shops, Museum, ATMs/Banks, Post Office **Gas (petrol) Station & Charging points.**

## Getting there by Ferry

- Passenger Ferry - To/From Gourock (28 miles from Glasgow)
www.calmac.co.uk

- Car Ferry - To/From McInroy's Point Gourock (30 miles from Glasgow)
www.western-ferries.co.uk

## Dunoon Highland Games

- Held in Late-August each year, this is the largest Highland gathering in the world. Tossing the Caber, Highland dancing, Athletics, and Pipe bands.
www.cowalgathering.com
*Argyll Road, Kirn, Dunoon.*

## Castle House Museum

- The history of the Cowal peninsula, from Neolithic times to wartime. Enjoy a picnic in the beautiful gardens with views over the Clyde.
https://castlehousemuseum.org.uk

# Isle of Bute

## Rothesay (Pop.6,000)
### (Pronounced Roth – Say)

Rothesay is the main town and Ferry Port on the Isle.

- Hotels, B&Bs, Food, Drink, Shops, Museum, ATMs/Banks, Post Office, buses & Taxis, **Gas (petrol) Station & Charging points.**

## Getting there by Ferry (32 miles from Glasgow)

- Passenger Ferry - To/From Weymss Bay (28 miles from Glasgow)
  www.calmac.co.uk

- Car Ferry - To/From Rhubodach,
  Bute/Colintraive,
  Cowal.
  www.calmac.co.uk

## Bute Highland Games

- Held in late-August each year.  Tossing the Caber, Highland dancing, Athletics, and Pipe bands.
  www.butehighlandgames.org
  *The Stadium, High Street.*

# Bute Museum

- The history of Bute from Mesolithic and Neolithic times through to the closing years of the 20th century.
  www.butemuseum.org.uk

# Rothesay Castle

- With a long association with the Stewart kings of Scotland.
  www.historicenvironment.scot

# Mount Stewart House (4 miles from Rothesay)

- Magnificent Victorian gothic mansion. Home to the Stuarts of Bute, descendants of the Royal House of Stuart.
  www.visitbute.com/mount-stuart-house

NW

# Back to the North and West
(From Lochgilphead To Oban, Fort William& Mallaig)

## The Dalriada Heritage Trail (3 Miles West from Lochgilphead)

- Linking the Crinan Canal, through ancient Atlantic oak woodlands with Achnabreac cup and ring marked rocks, Dunadd Fort, and the Moine Mhor National Nature Reserve through Kilmartin Glen (with standing stones and cairns) to Carnasserie Castle.

## Dunadd Fort (5 Miles North from Lochgilphead)

- Dating back 2,000 years, then latterly royal power center for Gaelic kings in the 500s to 800s AD.
  www.historicenvironment.scot

## Dunchraigaig Cairn (7 Miles North from Lochgilphead)

- 4,000-year-old Bronze age burial mound.
  www.historicenvironment.scot

## Nether Largie Standing Stones (7 Miles North from Lochgilphead)

- Dating back almost 5,000 years. Nearby are also "Temple Wood stone rings" and "Nether Largie South Cairn."
  www.britainexpress.com

## Kilmartin Village (8 Miles North from Lochgilphead)

- Here in Kilmartin Glen, there is one of the richest concentrations of prehistoric monuments and historical sites in Scotland. Containing over 800 monuments within a 6-mile radius.

## Kilmartin Museum

- With over 6, 000 years of History on display. Museum shop and a café.
  www.kilmartin.org

## Kilmartin Castle Hotel

- This 500-year-old Castle is now a luxury bed and breakfast venue.
  www.kilmartincastle.com

## Carnasserie Castle (9 Miles North from Lochgilphead)

- Ruined 15th century tower house located a mile north of Kilmartin.
  www.visitscotland.com

## Ardfern village (16 Miles North from Lochgilphead)

- Hotel (Galley of Lorne,17th Century Inn), B&Bs, Food, Drink, Craft Center with a tea-room, Shops, Buses and Yacht Benderloch Craignish was used the James Bond movie "From Russia with Love" for the motor-boat chase.

## Craignish Cruises (17 Miles North from Lochgilphead)

- A variety of tours available, with the trip to the whirlpool of Corryvreckan, the 3rd largest in the world a highlight. When the tide is right, its roar can be heard ten miles away.
  www.craignishcruises.co.uk

## Craobh Haven village (17 Miles North from Lochgilphead)

- Lord of the Isles Pub and Restaurant (live music), Shop, Yacht Center, Boat and Yacht Charters.

## Jenny Wren Boat Adventures (17 Miles North from Lochgilphead)

- A variety of tours available, with the trip to the whirlpool of Corryvreckan, the 3$^{rd}$ largest in the world a highlight. When the tide is right, its roar can be heard ten miles away. www.jennywrenboatcharter.com/boat-trips

## Lunga House Hotel (1 mile from Craobh Haven)

- 16$^{th}$ Century Tower House. www.lungahouse.co.uk

## Arduaine Garden (20 Miles South from Oban)

- Tranquil exotic garden on the coast. www.nts.org.uk/visit/places/arduaine-garden

## Clachan Bridge (The bridge over the Atlantic)
(12 Miles South from Oban)

- Old arched bridge (1793) joins the island of Seil
  to the mainland, spanning the Clachan Sound,
  which flows out of both ends into the Atlantic,
  giving it the nickname "The bridge over the
  Atlantic." As you cross the bridge, almost
  immediately on the right is an Inn called "Tigh
  an Truish" (Gaelic for The House of the
  Trousers). For a number of years after the
  1745 Jacobite rebellion the British Government
  had banned the wearing of the kilt (the Act of
  Proscription).
  So, any islanders going over to work on the
  mainland would change out of their kilts here
  and into trousers, then change back on their
  return back to the island.
  www.atlasobscura.com/places/clachan-
  bridge-bridge-over-atlantic

## The Scottish Slate Islands Heritage Trust
(17 Miles South from Oban, 4 miles South from the
Clachan Bridge)

- An interesting collection of artefacts and
  records relating to the social and industrial life
  of the Slate Islands of Argyll.
  https://slateislands.org.uk

**Easdale Island** (17 Miles South from Oban, 4 miles South from the Clachan Bridge)

- The World Stone Skimming Championships, held in late-September annually, open to the public. The island is reached by means of a 5-minute ferry from Ellenabeich on the Isle of Seil.
  www.stoneskimming.com

## Easdale Island Folk Museum

- Featuring local life and history, with genealogical information available.
  www.easdalemuseum.org

## The Puffer Bar, Restaurant and Tea-Room

- Award winning Bar & Restaurant on the tiny, car free island.
  http://pufferbarandrestaurant.co.uk

# Oban (Pop. 8,500)

For many people the town of Oban is a stopover on their way to somewhere else, like the Western Isles. And yes, it can be, but it is also somewhere that deserves a few days to enjoy the town and its surrounding area. We stayed at the "Lodge House" Hotel, and can highly recommend it, with great food, great views and great staff. Oban is known as the seafood capital of Scotland.

- Hotels, B&Bs, Food, Drink, Shops, Museum, ATMs/Banks, Post Office, Buses & Taxis, **Gas (petrol) Station & Charging points.**

## Getting there

- You can approach Oban by road from the South, East or North or you can get there by rail or bus.

## Ferries to/from Oban

- To/From – Castlebay (Barra), Coll, Colonsay, Craignure (Mull), Kennacraig, Lismore, Lochboisedale (South Uist), Mallaig, Port Askaig (Islay), Tiree. Kerrera (from Gallanach, a jetty 3 miles south of Oban, a five-minute trip).
www.calmac.co.uk

## Oban Airport

- Flights to/from the islands of Coll, Colonsay, Islay and Tiree.
  www.hebrideanair.co.uk

## Argyllshire Highland Games

- Held in Late-August each year.  Tossing the Caber, Highland dancing, Athletics, and Pipe bands.
  www.obangames.com
  *Mossfield Park, Oban.*

## Calmac Adventures

- Boat trip; From Oban, take the ferry to Mull, and then onwards to the tiny island of Ulva, lying just off Mull's west coast. From there, you'll continue on to Staffa.
  www.calmac.co.uk

## Lorne Highland Games

- Held in Late-June each year.  Tossing the Caber, Highland dancing, Athletics, and Pipe bands.
  http://lorne-highland-games.org.uk
  *Oban.*

## McCaig's Tower

- Looking like a Scottish version of the Roman Colosseum, sitting atop Battery hill is McCaig's Tower. With gardens inside and views all around, well worth the steps to the top.

## Oban Distillery (5th oldest distillery in Scotland).

- Pronunciation: Oh-bin.

- Name Origin: Gaelic - "Little bay."

- Established: 1794.

- Location: Stafford Street, Oban.

- Region: Highland.

- Visitor Center/Tours: Go to website for information.

- Website: www.malts.com/en-gb/visit-our-distilleries/oban

## Oban Games & Argyllshire Gathering

- Highland games. Held annually on the fourth Thursday in August. https://obanlive.com

## Oban Live

- Live music concert hosting the best of Scottish and international bands. Held annually in early June.
https://obanlive.com

## Oban War & Peace Museum

- Museum focusing on local life during peace and war.
www.obanmuseum.org.uk

# East from Oban

## St Conan's Kirk (21 miles East of Oban)

- A beautiful church in a beautiful setting. The Kirk was consecrated in 1930 but has incorporated many pieces from older churches. The window in the Bruce chapel comes from a church in Lieth which was built in 1483, the ossuary contains a bone of King Robert the Bruce, beams in the cloister come from two wrecked Battleships HMS Caledonia and HMS Duke of Wellington and there are pieces of Iona Abbey built into the walls.
  www.stconanskirk.org.uk
  *Lochawe, Dalmally.*

## Kilchurn Castle (23 miles East of Oban)

- One of the most photographed castles in Scotland. Built in the mid-1400s at the head of Loch Awe by Sir Colin Campbell, 1st Lord of Glenorchy.
  www.historicenvironment.scot
  *Lochawe, Dalmally.*

# We are about to take a detour to the Isles of Mull and Iona.

## To continue on the route North for Fort William and Mallaig see page 77.

# Isle of Mull (Pop. 3,000)

With 300 miles of coastline and a hilly interior, Mull is both wild and beautiful. You will probably recognize the main town of Tobermory, from the harbor's brightly painted houses, a favorite on social media.

You should probably fill your car in Oban before you head over to Mull as Gas/Petrol can be expensive on the isle. You have to travel through Mull to reach the nearby islands of Iona, Staffa (Fingal's Cave), and Ulva.

# Ferries

- To/From –Oban to Craignure (Mull).  Vehicle reservations are recommended.
  www.calmac.co.uk

- Iona to/from Fionnphort, Mull. On demand in the summer.

- Kilchoan, Ardnamurchan Peninsula to/from Tobermory, Mull.
  www.calmac.co.uk

- Lochaline, Morvern Peninsula to/from Fishnish, Mull.
  www.calmac.co.uk

- Ulva to/from Oskamull, Mull.  The ferry runs on demand.
  www.calmac.co.uk

# Tobermory (Pop. 1000)

If you have seen pictures of Scotland then you will probably recognize Tobermory's picture-perfect seafront, with the buildings painted in many bright colors.

- Hotels, B&Bs, Food, Drink, Shops, Aquarium, Museum, ATMs/Banks, Post Office, Buses & Taxis, **Gas (petrol) Station & Charging points.**

## Mull Aquarium

- Europe's first catch and release aquarium. All creatures spend a maximum of 4 weeks in the aquarium before being returned to the sea. This means the exhibits are constantly changed.
  www.mullaquarium.co.uk

## Mull Highland Games

- Held in Mid-July each year. Tossing the Caber, Highland dancing, Athletics, and Pipe bands.
  https://mullhighlandgames.weebly.com
  *Erray Park, Tobermory.*

## Mull Museum

- The history of the Isle of Mull.
  www.mullmuseum.org.uk

## Tobermory Distillery

- Pronunciation: Toe-Ber-More-ay.

- Name Origin: Gaelic - "Mary's well."

- Established: 1798.

- Location: Tobermory, Isle of Mull.

- Region: Island.

- Visitor Center/Tours: Go to website for information.

- Website: https://tobermorydistillery.com

## Staffa Tours

- Boat trips leaving from Tobermory (Mull), Fionnphort (Mull) and Iona to the isle of Staffa and Fingal's Cave.
  www.staffatours.com

## Staffa Trips

- Boat trips leaving from Fionnphort (Mull) and Iona to the isle of Staffa and Fingal's Cave. www.staffatrips.co.uk

## Glengorm Castle Hotel (5 miles from Tobermory)

- Dating from 1860, in the Scottish Baronial style. www.glengormcastle.co.uk *Glengorm Castle, Tobermory.*

## Craignure (21 miles from Tobermory)

- Village and main ferry terminal. Hotel, B&Bs, Food, Drink, Shop, Car Hire, Post Office, Buses, **Charging points.**

## Duart Castle (24 miles from Tobermory, 2 miles from Craignure)

- The seat of the Maclean family for the last 700 years. https://duartcastle.com

# Iona (Pop. Less than 200)

The island is only 3.5 miles long by 1.5 miles wide, with the main settlement of "Baile Mor" (meaning "big town") consisting of a few cottages. The main reason tourist come to Iona is to see the Abbey founded by St Columba and built in 563. Cars are not allowed on Iona and the car park next to the ferry terminal in Fionnphort (Mull) is expensive. There is however a free car park at the back of Fionnphort village, but it's small and fills up quickly during the summer. Limited accommodation is available on Iona.

- B&Bs, Food, Drink, Shop, Museum, Post Office, Taxi (one).

## Ferries

- Iona to/from Fionnphort, Mull. On demand in the summer.

## Iona Abbey

- 6th century abbey founded by St Columba and where the famous "Book of Kells" was written
- (the book is now held at Trinity College Library, Dublin).  The Abbey Museum houses Scotland's finest collection of early medieval carved stones and crosses. www.historicenvironment.scot

## Iona Heritage Center

- Showcasing island life over the last few centuries; the fishing and crofting community, artists, churches, craftworkers, and memorable events.  With a café and gift shop. www.ionaheritage.co.uk

## Staffa Tours

- Boat trips leaving from Tobermory (Mull), Fionnphort (Mull) and Iona to the isle of Staffa and Fingal's Cave. www.staffatours.com

## Staffa Trips

- Boat trips leaving from Fionnphort (Mull) and Iona to the isle of Staffa and Fingal's Cave. www.staffatrips.co.uk

# We now rejoin the route North from Oban to Fort William.

## Dunstaffnage Castle and Chapel (4 miles North from Oban)

- A MacDougal clan stronghold built around 1240 and taken by Robert the Bruce in 1308. Its most famous prisoner has to be Flora MacDonald held here in 1746 before being sent to the Tower of London for helping Bonnie Prince Charlie evade the Redcoats after Culloden.
  www.historicenvironment.scot

## Castle Stalker (18 miles North from Oban)

- Iconic 15th century castle set in the middle of a Loch the castle is privately owned, but a limited number of tours are available by prior appointment. Go to website for details.
  www.castlestalker.com

# Glencoe Village

(34 miles North from Oban, 17 miles from Fort William)

Named for the stunning Glen in which it sits and well known for the massacre of the Macdonalds on the 13 Feb 1692 by government troops.

- Hotels, B&Bs, Food, Drink, Shop, Buses& Taxis, **Gas/Petrol & Charging points.**

## Glencoe folk Museum (34 miles North from Oban, 17 miles from Fort William)

- Set within traditional 18th century heather-thatched cottages, Glencoe Folk Museum holds an eclectic array of objects celebrating local heritage and history. A 3-minute walk will get you to the Glencoe Memorial. www.glencoemuseum.com

## Glencoe Memorial (34 miles North from Oban, 17 miles from Fort William)

- Memorial to remember the 38 Macdonald's massacred by British government soldiers on the13 Feb 1692.

# Glencoe Outdoor Center

- Activities (depending on the season) include skiing, hill walking, climbing & abseiling, archery, orienteering, sailing, windsurfing, kayaking, and canoeing.
www.glencoeoutdoorcentre.org.uk

# Glencoe Visitor Center (35 miles North from Oban, 16 miles from Fort William)

- National Trust for Scotland visitor center, with information on the area.
https://discoverglencoe.scot

# Fort William (Pop. 10,500)

The town sits under the tallest mountain in the UK, Ben Nevis. Hiking to the top of Ben Nevis is a popular thing to do but be aware on a nice day it can take you 5 hours to get to the top. The path is rough (wear good shoes) and the weather can change, this is not to be taken lightly.
Fort William is known as the Outdoor capital of Scotland with lots of activities (depending on the season) that include skiing, hill walking, climbing (indoor and outdoor & abseiling, orienteering, archery, wind surfing, paddle boarding, biking, sailing, kayaking, and canoeing. Fort William is the start/Finish of the West Highland Way (97-mile hike from Milngavie, Glasgow) long distance walking route and also the start/Finish of the Great Glen Way (84-mile hike to Inverness) long distance walking route, I have hiked both routes (the WHW 7 times) and have written a guide to both.

- Hotels, B&Bs, Food, Drink, Shops, Museum, ATMs/Banks, Car Hire, Buses, Taxis, Post Office **Gas/petrol Station & Charging points.**

## Getting there

- You can approach Fort William by road from the South, East or North or you can get there by rail or bus.

There is a wealth of accommodations to be had in and around town, and out in the countryside (all fall within the area marked on the map).
We have stayed at the following hotels and would happily recommend all of them;

## Distillery Guest house

- Three former distillery workers cottages converted into a hotel. When we arrived, they gave us a glass of Whisky.
www.distilleryguesthouse.com

## Lime Tree an Ealdhain

- Historic 1850 former Church Manse building overlooking the Loch in the center of Fort William
www.limetreefortwilliam.co.uk

## Nevis Bank Inn

- Modern **hotel** situated 10 minutes' walk from the high street and the train station.
www.nevisbankinn.co.uk

## Factor's Inn & Cottage (3 miles from Fort William)

- On Inverlochy Estate, staying here gives you access to the Castle Hotel (Restaurant, high Tea etc.) at about a fifth of the price of staying at the castle.
  https://factorsinn.com


## The Moorings, Banavie (3 miles from Fort William)

- Situated on the banks of the Caledonian Canal at the famous Neptune's staircase locks. Just five minutes' drive from Fort William town center but a million miles away from the everyday hustle and bustle.
  https://moorings-fortwilliam.co.uk

# While Hiking the Great Glen Way from Fort William to Inverness.

**Aoanach Mor Hotel, Spean Bridge** (9 miles from Fort William)

- Situated in the village of Spean Bridge, this is a delightful family-run hotel.
  www.aonachmorhotel.co.uk

**Glengarry Castle Hotel** (24 miles from Fort William)

- This 19th century country house sits in 60 acres on Loch Oich.
  www.glengarry.net

**The Inch Hotel, Fort Augustus** (24 miles from Fort William)

- The Inchnacardoch House was built by Lord Lovat as a hunting lodge over 150-years-ago.
  https://inchhotel.com

**Glenmoriston Arms Hotel** (38 miles from Fort William)

- A stone's throw from Loch Ness in the picturesque Highland village of Invermoriston. http://glenmoristonarms.co.uk

**Urquhart Castle** (48 miles East from Fort William)

- Dating way back tó its start as a Pictish fort, this huge castle sits on a promontory dominating Loch Ness. www.historicenvironment.scot *Drumnadrochit, Inverness.*

**Loch Ness Lodge** (51 miles East from Fort William)

- This hotel (built in 1740) is located in the village of Drumnadrochit close to Loch Ness. We stayed here while hiking the Great Glen Way and can recommend it. www.lochnesslodgehotels.co.uk *Drumnadrochit.*

# While Hiking the West Highland Way from Milngavie (Glasgow) to Fort William.

**Clachaig Inn, Ballachuilish** (20 miles from Fort William)

- Very popular with hikers and climbers. Dating back at least to 1864, this inn has a huge range of **Scottish craft ales**, lagers, stouts and ciders, with a collection of over **400 malt whiskies,** over **130 Scottish distilled gins** amongst and ever-growing list of **Scottish rums, vodkas and other spirits.**
https://clachaig.com

**Bridge of Orchy Hotel** (40 miles from Fort William)

- The Hotel has 32 rooms decorated in a traditional style and overlook the surrounding countryside.
www.bridgeoforchy.co.uk

## The Drovers Inn (57 miles from Fort William)

- The inn is over 300 years old and very likely had the famous Scottish outlaw Rob Roy as a patron, as this was the area from which he came.
  www.droversinn.co.uk

## Crannog Cruises

- Leisurely cruises on Loch Linne.
  https://fortwilliamseatours.co.uk

## Fort William Sea Tours

- Powerboat "Seafaris" on Loch Linne.
  https://fortwilliamseatours.co.uk

## Jacobite Steam Train

- One of the most iconic train journeys in the world and of course made famous as the "Hogwarts Express" in the Harry Potter Movies.
  https://westcoastrailways.co.uk/jacobite/steam-train-trip

## West Highland Museum

- Telling the story of the region and its history. With a collection relating to Bonnie Prince Charlie and the Jacobite cause. www.westhighlandmuseum.org.uk

## Ben Nevis Distillery (2 miles North from Fort William)

- Pronunciation: Ben - Nevis.

- Name Origin: The highest mountain (Ben Nevis) in Scotland is next to the distillery.

- Established: 1825.

- Location: Lochy Bridge, Fort William.

- Region: Highland.

- Visitor Center/Tours: Go to website for information.

- Website: www.bennevisdistillery.com

## Inverlochy Castle Hotel (3 miles North from Fort William)

- This 19th century castle sits amongst the foothills of Scotland's highest mountain - the mighty Ben Nevis.
  https://inverlochycastlehotel.com
  *Torlundy, Fort William.*


## Active Highs (22 miles North from Fort William)

- Outdoor Center with; Canyoning, Gorge Walking, Kayak Trips, Climbing & Abseiling, and White-Water Rafting.
  www.activehighs.co.uk
  *The Great Glen Hostel, South Laggan, Spean Bridge.*

# East from Fort William

## Glengarry Highland Games (16 miles East from Fort William)

- Held in Late-July each year. Tossing the Caber, Highland dancing, Athletics, and Pipe bands.
  https://glengarryhighlandgames.com
  *A87, Invergarry.*

## Glenurquhart Highland Games (51 miles East from Fort William)

- Held in Late-August each year. Tossing the Caber, Highland dancing, Athletics, and Pipe bands.
  www.glenurquhart-highland-games.co.uk
  *Drumnadrochit, Inverness.*

# West from Fort William

## Neptune's Staircase (3 miles West from Fort William)

- A flight of 8 Locks on the Caledonian Canal at Banavie.
  www.scottishcanals.co.uk/locations/neptunes-staircase

## Treasures of the Earth (4 miles West from Fort William)

- Museum with a unique collection of crystals and gems.
  https://treasuresoftheearth.co.uk

## Glenfinnan Monument (17 miles West from Fort William)

- A monument to those that fell during the Jacobite rising of 1545/6. Glenfinnan is where Bonnie Prince Charlie raised his standard to start the rebellion. Standing at the head of Loch Shiel and set in stunning highland scenery, this is well worth your time. Also, just opposite is the famous Glenfinnan Viaduct, made famous in the Harry Potter films.
www.nts.org.uk/visit/places/glenfinnan-monument
*Glenfinnan.*

## Glenfinnan Highland Games (17 miles West from Fort William)

- Held in Late-August each year. Tossing the Caber, Highland dancing, Athletics, and Pipe bands.
www.glenfinnan.org.uk/gathering.asp
*Games Field, Glenfinnan.*

## Glenfinnan Station Museum (17 miles West from Fort William)

- Telling the story/history of the West Highland railway.
https://glenfinnanstationmuseum.co.uk
*Glenfinnan.*

## Glenfinnan Viaduct (17 miles West from Fort William)

- Made famous in the Harry Potter films. *Glenfinnan.*

## Arisaig Sea Kayak Center (36 miles North/West from Fort William)

- As the name suggests, offering Sea kayak adventures.
  https://arisaigseakayakcentre.co.uk
  *Arisaig.*

## Arisaig Highland Games & Clan Donald Gathering (36 miles North/West from Fort William)

- Held in Late-July each year. Tossing the Caber, Highland dancing, Athletics, and Pipe bands.
  www.arisaighighlandgames.co.uk
  *Arisaig.*

### Mallaig & Morar Highland Games (40 miles North/West from Fort William)

- Held in Early-August each year. Tossing the Caber, Highland dancing, Athletics, and Pipe bands.
www.facebook.com/MallaigAndMorarHighland Games
*Lovat Field, Morar.*

# Mallaig (Pop. 800)
### (43 miles North/West from Fort William)

Mallaig is the main fishing port, a major ferry hub and the Rail terminus on the West coast of Scotland.

- Hotels, B&Bs, Food, Drink, Shops, Medical Center, Museum, ATM/Bank, e-bike hire, Buses, Post Office **Gas/petrol Station & Charging points.**

## Getting there

- You can only approach Mallaig by road from the South/East or you can get there by rail or ferry. Scotrail provides a good service between Glasgow Queen Street to Fort William and Mallaig.

# Ferries

- To/From Armadale, Isle of Skye.
  www.calmac.co.uk

- To/From Inverie, Knoydart Peninsula.
  www.calmac.co.uk

- To/From Inverie, Knoydart Peninsula.
  https://westernislescruises.co.uk

- To/From Lochboisdale, South Uist.
  www.calmac.co.uk

- To/From Oban.
  www.calmac.co.uk

- To/From the Isle of Eigg.
  www.calmac.co.uk

- To/From the Isle of Canna.
  www.calmac.co.uk

- To/From the Isle of Muck.
  www.calmac.co.uk

- To/From the Isle of Rum.
  www.calmac.co.uk

- To/From Tarbet.
  https://westernislescruises.co.uk

## Mallaig Heritage Center

- Telling the story of West Lochaber, its people and landscape. Think Picts, Vikings and Scots.
  www.mallaigheritage.org.uk

## Minch Adventures

- Opportunities to see whales, dolphins, seal colonies & sea eagles.
  www.minchadventures.co.uk

# Chapter 3

## Skye and the Outer Hebrides

# Isle of Skye (Pop. 10,000)

You can either cross over the Skye Bridge or get there by Ferry, I have done both.  Arriving by ferry and leaving over the bridge.

The first night we stayed at the Rosedale hotel in Portree, which overlooks the harbor and was formerly three Fishermen's cottages.  Our second night on Skye, we stayed at Kinloch Lodge, Sleat.

Skye is 639 sq. miles in area, but everything is less than 45 miles away from Portree.

Beautiful scenery, lots of wildlife and incredible seafood are all available here.

## Getting there;

- Bridge from Kyle of Lochalsh – Kyleakin (Skye)

- Glenelg – Skye Ferry (Small with limited capacity.
  https://skyeferry.co.uk

- Mallaig – Armadale (Skye)
  www.calmac.co.uk/article/2982/Skye-Mallaig---Armadale

## Things to do and see;

On our last trip, we caught the Ferry from Mallaig on the mainland to Armadale on Skye.
We did a circular tour around the island (by car), travelling counterclockwise.
The first night we stayed at the Rosedale hotel in Portree, which overlooks the harbor and was formerly three Fishermen's cottages.
Our second night on Skye, we stayed at Kinloch Lodge, Sleat. Leaving over the bridge to the mainland.

## Armadale Castle, Gardens & Museum (42 miles from Portree)

- Unfortunately, the castle was ravaged by fire and only the shell remains, but the gardens make for a great walk and the museum is well worth a visit. www.armadalecastle.com

## Torabhaig Distillery (38 miles from Portree)

- Pronunciation: To-ra-vaig.

- Name Origin: Named for the farm on which it was built.

- Established:2014.

- Location: Teangue, Isle of Skye.

- Region: Island.

- Visitor Center/Tours: Go to website for information.

- Website: www.torabhaig.com

# Harapool & Broadford villages
## (26 miles from Portree)

These two villages almost meld into one, they are so close together and they have;

- Hotels, B&Bs, Food, Drink, shops, ATMs/Banks, Post Office, Medical Center & **Gas (petrol) Station**.

# Portree (Pop. 2,500)

The village of Portree (Port Ruighe in Gaelic) is the capital of Skye.

- Hotels, B&Bs, Food, Drink, shops, Car Hire, Bike Hire, ATMs/Banks, Post Office, **Gas (petrol) & Charging Stations**.

## Isle of Skye Highland Games

- Held in Early-August each year. Tossing the Caber, Highland dancing, Athletics, and Pipe bands.
  www.skye-highland-games.co.uk
  *Portree.*

## Isle of Skye Pipe band (Portree)

- Play every Tuesday evening in Somerled Square during the summer. www.spanglefish.com/isleofskyepipeband

## The old Man of Storr (6 miles from Portree)

- The most famous (and busiest) walk on Skye, to one of the world's most photographed landscapes.

## Kilt Rock & Mealt Falls (15 miles from Portree)

- Kilt Rock gets its name from the 90-meter-high Basalt rock cliff face that resemble the pleats in a kilt.

## Quirang (19 miles from Portree)

- This can be hiked, but is quite difficult, with stunning scenery. In an area known as Trotternish.

# You are about to turn around the top of the isle and the distances back to Portree will lessen.

## The Skye Museum of Island life (22 miles from Portree)

- Giving an insight to island life 100-years-ago, well worth a visit.
  www.skyemuseum.co.uk

## Flora McDonald's Grave

- Next to the Skye Museum of Island life.
  *"Her name will be mentioned in history and if courage and fidelity be virtues, mentioned with honour."*
  Alexander McQueen the famous fashion icon is also buried here.

# **Uig** (16 miles from Portree)

- Village with; Food, drink, shop, Post Office & **Gas (petrol) Station.**

## **Fairy Glen** (16 miles from Portree)

- Lovely landscape, which makes it easy to believe that Fairies inhabit the area.

# **Just after the village of Borve, take the A850** (Turn right) **to carry-on around the isle.**

## **Dunvegan Castle** (22 miles from Portree)

- The Castle is the oldest continuously inhabited castle in Scotland and has been the ancestral home of the Chiefs of clan MacLeod for 800 years. www.dunvegancastle.com
  *MacLeod Estate, Dunvegan.*

# Dunvegan
### (20 miles from Portree)

- Village with shops & **Gas (petrol) Station.**

# Possible Side Trip from Dunvegan

## Three Chimneys Restaurant (5 miles from Dunvegan castle)

- Eating lunch here was our first experience of a Michelin starred restaurant and the price reflected it. But the food was stellar, as was the service. While we were waiting for our food, I looked out the window and saw Dolphins/Porpoises playing in Loch Dunvegan.
www.threechimneys.co.uk

**Neist Point Lighthouse** (6 miles from The Three Chimney's)

- About a 45-minute-walk (round-trip) from the car park to one of Scotland's most famous and picturesque lighthouses.

# Back to the route around Skye

**Lonmore village** (11 miles from Neist Point Lighthouse)

- At the village, turn right onto the A863 to carry-on around the isle.

# Back to the route South

**Talisker Distillery** (19 miles from Lonmore)

- Pronunciation: Tal-isk-er

- Name Origin: Gaelic - "Sloping rock."

- Established: 1831.

- Location: Carbost, Isle of Skye.

- Region: Island.

- Visitor Center/Tours: Go to website for information.

- Website: www.malts.com/en-row/our-whisky-collection/talisker

## Fairy Pools (20 miles from Portree)

- Beautiful pools that you can swim in (if you like really cold water) or you could just take some stunning photos.

## Kinloch Lodge

- We finished our tour of Skye here, where we had dinner and stayed the night. The restaurant was also Michelin starred and again the food was superb and relatively inexpensive as it was rolled into the cost of the room.
  https://kinloch-lodge.co.uk

# Outer Hebrides
(Western Isles)

## Hebridean Whisky Trail Festival

- Held in Late-May each year. With 4 distilleries situated on different Hebridean islands. https://hebrideanwhisky.com

## HebCelt Festival

- Four-day Traditional Celtic Music Festival usually held in July at various venues on the Hebrides. www.hebceltfest.com

All the major islands are connected to each other by bridges or ferries. The Hebrides are famous for their white sandy beaches. If, you are travelling by car you must book your Ferry ticket in advance.

The remote locations, small populations and lack of light pollution on these islands make for great star gazing and viewing the northern lights (best in winter).

There is ample opportunity to walk/hike or bike and see the beautiful scenery, view the wildlife and work up an appetite for some incredible seafood.

I have laid out the Islands as you see them on a map, starting at the top with;

- Lewis
- Harris
- Berneray
- North Uist
- Benbecula
- South Uist
- Eriskay
- Barra

# Isle of Lewis (Pop. 19,000)

The isles of Lewis (Northern) and Harris (Southern) are in fact one island, the largest in Scotland. Until the 20th century there were no roads between Lewis and Harris, because of the mountains on the island.
The only way to get from Lewis to Harris was by sea, hence them being classed as two separate islands. The isle of Lewis/Harris covers 841 sq. miles and for distances around the Isle, I am assuming a start point of Stornoway as it is the main town and ferry port of the isle.

## Getting there, Stornoway Airport;

- From Benbecula, Edinburgh, Glasgow and Inverness (Logan Air)
  www.hial.co.uk/stornoway-airport

## By Ferry

- From Ullapool to Stornoway.

- Oban to Lochboisdale, Isle of South Uist
  www.calmac.co.uk

# Stornoway (Pop. 6,000)

The main town and port.

- Hotels, B&Bs, Food, Drink, Car Hire, Shops, ATMs/Banks, Post Office, **Gas (petrol) & Charging Stations**.

## Bosta House

- Reconstruction of an Iron Age house found nearby. Guides are on hand to explain what it was like to live there.
  https://berneramuseum.wixsite.com

## HebCelt Festival

- Four-day Traditional Celtic Music Festival usually held in July at various venues on the Hebrides.
  www.hebceltfest.com

## Lewis Castle & Museum

- Built in 1847 and now home to the famous Lewis chessmen. Offering self-catering and hotel rooms.
  www.lews-castle.co.uk
  *Stornoway.*

## The Blackhouse Arnol (15 miles from Stornoway)

- A "Blackhouse" was the standard type of house the islanders lived in around 100-years-ago. Close to Dun Carloway Broch, Callanish Standing Stones and Gearrannan Blackhouse Village and Shawbost Norse Mill and Kiln.

## Callinish Standing Stones (17 miles from Stornoway)

- Impressive 5,000-year-old stone circle. Close to Dun Carloway Broch, Gearrannan Blackhouse Village and Shawbost Norse Mill and Kiln. www.historicenvironment.scot/visit-a-place/places/calanais-standing-stones

## Dun Carloway Broch (18 miles from Stornoway)

- Stone tower built circa 200 BC. Close to Callanish Standing Stones, Gearrannan Blackhouse Village and Shawbost Norse Mill and Kiln. www.historicenvironment.scot/visit-a-place/places/dun-carloway

## Gearrannan Blackhouse (18 miles from Stornoway)

- Village and living Museum with self-catering accommodation. Close to Callanish Standing Stones, Dun Carloway Broch, and Shawbost Norse Mill and Kiln.
  www.gearrannan.com

## Shawbost Norse Mill and Kiln (19 miles from Stornoway)

- Close to Dun Carloway Broch, Callanish Standing Stones and Gearrannan Blackhouse Village.

## Abhainn Dearg Distillery (36 miles from Stornoway)

- Pronunciation: Aveen Jarraek.

- Name Origin: Gaelic - "Red River."

- Established: 2008.

- Location: Carnish, Isle of Lewis.

- Region: Island.

- Visitor Center/Tours: Go to website for information.

- Website: www.abhainndearg.co.uk

**Uig historical society Museum** (33 miles from Stornoway)

- Local Historical Society Museum with several displays covering different aspects of local history. www.ceuig.co.uk

# Isle of Harris (Pop. 21,000)

The isles of Lewis (Northern) and Harris (Southern) are in fact one island, the largest in Scotland. Until the 20th century there were no roads between Lewis and Harris, because of the mountains on the island. The only way to get from Lewis to Harris was by sea, hence them being classed as two separate islands. The isle of Lewis/Harris covers 841 sq. miles and for distances around the Isle, I am assuming a start point of Tarbert as it is the main town and ferry port of the isle.

## Getting there, Stornoway Airport;

- From Benbecula, Edinburgh, Glasgow and Inverness (Logan Air) www.hial.co.uk/stornoway-airport

## By Ferry

- From Uig, Isle of Skye to Tarbert. www.calmac.co.uk

# Tarbert (Pop. 500)

The main town and port.

- Hotels, B&Bs, Food, Drink, Car Hire, Shops, ATMs/Banks, Post Office, **Gas (petrol) & Charging Stations**.

## Amhuinnsuidhe Castle Hotel (6 miles from Tarbert)

- Built in 1865 in the Scottish Baronial style. http://amhuinnsuidhe-com.stackstaging.com *Amhuinnsuidh.*

## Bunavoneader Whaling Station (4 miles from Tarbert)

- No longer active, some remains can be seen like the Chimney and a few Whale bones. www.virtualheb.co.uk/whaling-station-isle-of-harris

## Isle of Harris Distillery

- Pronunciation: Isle-of-Harris.

- Name Origin: Named for the Island where it is situated.

- Established: 2015.

- Location: Tarbert, Isle of Harris.

- Region: Island.

- Visitor Center/Tours: Go to website for information.

- Website: https://harrisdistillery.com

## Shawbost

- Harris Tweed Mill and shop.
  www.harristweedhebrides.com

## St Clemens Church (6 miles from Tarbert)

- Built in the early 1500s, built as the burial place of the Clan MacLeod.
  www.historicenvironment.scot

# Isle of Berneray (Pop. 137)

Covering an area of only around 6 sq. miles. There is a bus service from the isle of Berneray in the North, down through North Uist, Benbecula, and South Uist to the isle of Eriskay in the South, with causeways linking the islands.

The isle is probably best known for its beaches and coves, the West beach is 3 miles of un-spoilt sand.

If you wish to see the Northern lights, this is one of the best places to go, with no light pollution they can easily be seen (mainly in Winter).

# Isle of North Uist (Pop. 1200)

The isle stretches 20 miles north-south, 25 miles east-west.  For distances around the Isle, I am assuming a start point of Lochmaddy as it is the main village and ferry port of the isle.  No car hire on the island, but you can book a car from Benbecula airport and have it dropped off, to meet you at the ferry.  Taxis and minibuses are available, as well as the regular islands bus service.

## Getting there, Benbecula Airport;

Benbecula is the small isle Lying between North and South Uist and linked to both by road causeways.

- From Glasgow, Inverness and Stornoway (Logan Air)
  www.hial.co.uk/benbecula-airport

## By Ferry

- From Uig, Isle of Skye to Lochmaddy.
  www.calmac.co.uk

## Lochmaddy

- The main town and port.  Hotels, B&Bs, Food, Drink, Shops, ATMs, Post Office, **Gas (petrol) & Charging Stations**.

## Camera Obscura (Hut of the Shadows)

- Go on a sunny day to see a projected view of Lochmaddy.

## Taigh Chearsabhagh Museum & Arts Center

- Local art center, shop, Cafe and Post Office. www.taigh-chearsabhagh.org

## Barpa Langass (6 miles from Lochmaddy)

- A 5000-year-old burial chamber. A short walk away is Pobull Fhinn.

## Pobull Fhinn (6.5 miles from Lochmaddy)
- Stone circle from around 2,000BC. A short walk away is Barpa Langass.

## The Hebridean Smokehouse (8 miles from Lochmaddy)

- With a long tradition of peat-smoking delicious seafood. www.hebrideansmokehouse.com *Clachan.*

# Isle of Benbecula (Pop. 1300)

The small isle Lying between North and South Uist and linked to both by road causeways.
The isle stretches 7 miles north-south and 7 miles east-west.  Car hire is available at the airport, best to pre-book.

## Getting there, Benbecula Airport;

- From Glasgow, Inverness and Stornoway (Logan Air)
  www.hial.co.uk/benbecula-airport

# Balivanich

The main village.

- Hotel, B&Bs, Self-Catering, Food, Drink, Shops, ATM/Bank, Post Office, **Gas (petrol) & Charging Stations**.

# Isle of South Uist (Pop. 1800)

The isle stretches 25 miles north-south and 5 miles east-west. For distances around the Isle, I am assuming a start point of Lochboisedale as it is the main village and ferry port of the isle. South Uist is linked by a causeway to Eriskay in the South and to North Uist in the North.

## Getting there, Benbecula Airport;

Benbecula is the small isle Lying between North and South Uist and linked to both by road causeways.

- From Glasgow, Inverness and Stornoway (Logan Air)
  www.hial.co.uk/benbecula-airport

## By Ferry

- From Castlebay, Barra to Lochboisedale.

- From Mallaig to Lochboisedale.

- Oban to Lochboisdale.
  www.calmac.co.uk

# Lochboisedale

The main Village and Port.

- Hotel, B&Bs, Self-Catering, Food, Drink, Shops, ATM/Bank.

## South Uist Highland Gathering

- Held in Late-July each year.  Tossing the Caber, Highland dancing, Athletics, and Pipe bands.
  www.shottshighlandgames.org.uk
  *Askernish Machair, Nr Lochboisdale, South Uist, Outer Hebrides*

## Kildonan (7 miles Lochboisdale)

- Flora MacDonald's Birthplace.

- Museum with café and shop.
  https://kildonanmuseum.co.uk

## Our Lady of the Isles (16 miles Lochboisdale)

- 30ft high statue in granite of the Madonna and Child.

# Isle of Eriskay (Pop. 130)

The isle stretches 2.8 miles long north to south and 1.6 miles wide and is linked by a causeway to South Uist.
In 1941, the SS Politician ran aground in the waters between South Uist and Eriskay, with a cargo of whisky. This was the basis for the book and film Whisky Galore and the only pub on the island is called the "Politician" (food and drink). The island is also known for its native Eriskay Ponies.
There are several B&Bs on the island.

## By Ferry

- From Barra to Lochboisedale.
  www.calmac.co.uk

# Eriskay

The main Village.

- Hotel, B&Bs, Self-Catering, Food, Drink, Shops, Post Office.

# Isle of Barra (Pop. 1100)

The isle is 11 miles long and 6 miles wide.  For distances around the Isle, I am assuming a start point of Castlebay as it is the main village and main ferry port of the isle. Buses, Taxis, Car and Bike hire are available.  Hotels and B&Bs are available throughout the isle.
The main road (A888) is circular and there are signs to monuments and villages.

## Getting there, Barra Airport (9 miles from Castlebay)

- From Glasgow (Logan Air)
  Barra Airport is one of the last in the world that still uses a beach as its runway.  A siren sounds when an aircraft is coming into land and you need to get clear of the beach.
  www.hial.co.uk/barra-airport

## By Ferry

- From Oban to Castlebay, Isle of Barra.

- From Eriskay to Ardmhòr, Isle of Barra.
  www.calmac.co.uk

# Castlebay Village

- Hotel, B&Bs, Food, Drink, Hospital, Bank/ATM, Shops and **Gas (petrol) & Charging Stations.**

## Dun Cuier (4.5 miles from Castlebay) & Dun Bharpa (4.2 miles from Castlebay)

- Old ruined hill forts (Brochs), of the two Dun Cuier is the better preserved. Access to both involves walking over rough ground and a bit of an ascent, with Dun Cuier the shorter walk.

## Hebridean Toffee Company

- Gift shop and café with deck overlooking the bay.
  www.hebrideantoffeecompany.com
  *Castlebay.*

## Isle of Barra Distillery

- Makers of "Atlantic Gin."
  www.isleofbarradistillers.com
  *Castlebay.*

## Kisimul Castle (late 15<sup>th</sup> century)

- A 5-minute boat trip from Castlebay and open from April to September. The seat of the chief of Clan MacNeil.
  *Castlebay.*


## St Barr's Church (9.5 miles from Castlebay)

- Now a ruin, but in the north chapel is a full-size replica of an elaborate Norse rune stone which was found in the cemetery in 1865.
  On one side the runic inscription reads "After Thorgerth, Steiner's daughter, this cross was raised," on the other side is an elaborate Celtic cross with plaited interlace.
  There are also three 16th century grave-slabs in this chapel believed to have once covered the graves of the MacNeils.
  www.visitouterhebrides.co.uk
  *1 Cille Bharra, Eoligarry.*

# Isle of Vatersay (Pop. 90)

The isle is only 3 miles from north to south, the northern section of the island is about 3 ½ miles from west to east and is linked by a causeway to Barra.
Accommodation; One self-catering cottage.

## Dun a' Chaolais

- Remains of a Broch (fortified house/tower).

# Chapter 4

## Stay in a Castle or Stately Home.

# Near Fort William

**Glengarry Castle Hotel** (24 miles from the town center)

- This 19th century country house sits in 60 acres on Loch Oich.
  www.glengarry.net
  *Glengarry.*

**Inverlochy Castle Hotel** (3 miles from the town center)

- This 19th century castle sits amongst the foothills of Scotland's highest mountain - the mighty Ben Nevis.
  https://inverlochycastlehotel.com
  *Torlundy, Fort William.*

## Mingary Castle Hotel (67 miles from the town center)

- This 13th century Castle stands atop a rocky outcrop above the Sound of Mull.
  www.ardnamurchanestate.co.uk/blog/mingary-castle
  *Arisaig.*

## The Inch Hotel (33 miles from Fort William)

- Inchnacardoch the former hunting lodge of Lord Lovat on the shores of Loch Ness.
  https://inchhotel.com
  *Fort Augustus, Inverness-shire.*

## Cameron House Hotel (25 miles from George Square)

- Baronial Mansion sitting on the "Bonnie, Bonnie banks" of Loch Lomond.
  www.cameronhouse.co.uk
  *Alexandria, Loch Lomond.*

## Castle Levan Hotel (32 miles from George Square)

- Castle Levan was built circa 1457. B&B accommodation in 2 guest bedchambers.
  www.castle-levan.com
  *Gourock.*

# Near Oban

**Barcaldine Castle Hotel** (10 miles from the town center)

- 17th century tower house castle with breakfast accommodation.
  www.barcaldinecastle.co.uk
  *Benderloch.*

**Lunga House Hotel** (23 Miles South from Oban)

- 16th Century Tower House.
  www.lungahouse.co.uk
  *Craob haven.*

**Kilmartin Castle Hotel** (29 miles from the town center)

- This 500-year-old Castle is now a luxury bed and breakfast venue.
  www.kilmartincastle.com
  *Kilmartin, Lochgilphead.*

# Near Portree (Isle of Skye)

## Kinloch Lodge Hotel (33 miles from Portree)

- Lord Macdonald's former hunting lodge on the shores of Loch Na Dal.
  https://kinloch-lodge.co.uk
  *Sleat, Isle of Skye.*

## Skeabost Lodge

- A 19th century hunting lodge, built in 1871.
  www.skeabosthotel.com
  *Portree.*

# Near Stornoway

## Lews Castle & Museum

- Built in 1847 and now home to the famous Lewis chessmen. Offering self-catering and hotel rooms.
  www.lews-castle.co.uk
  *Stornoway.*

# Near Tarbert (Isle of Harris)

## Amhuinnsuidhe Castle Hotel (6 miles from the town center)

- Built in 1865 in the Scottish Baronial style.
  http://amhuinnsuidhe-com.stackstaging.com
  *Amhuinnsuidh.*

## Stonefield Castle Hotel (2 miles from Tarbert)

- Scottish baronial styled castle dating back to 1837.
  www.bespokehotels.com/stonefieldcastle
  *Stonefield, Tarbert.*

# Near Tobermory (Isle of Mull)

## Glengorm Castle Hotel (5 miles from the town center)

- Dating from 1860, in the Scottish Baronial style.
  www.glengormcastle.co.uk
  *Glengorm Castle, Tobermory.*

# Chapter 5

## Festivals and Celebrations

Listed by month, so you can find them or avoid them, your choice.

# January

### Burns Night

- Held all over Scotland and indeed all over the world to celebrate the birthday (25 January 1759) of the Scots poet Robert Burns. With poetry readings, haggis, kilts and whisky. www.scotland.org

# May

### Campbeltown Malts Festival

- Held annually every May. A 3-day celebration of Glengyle, Glen Scotia and Springbank. Campbeltown's 3 whisky distilleries. www.explorecampbeltown.com

## Feis Ile

- Islay Festival with; Ceilidhs, Gaelic lessons, Golf, Music, Poetry and Whisky. Held annually in late May.
  www.islayfestival.com

## Hebridean Whisky Trail Festival

- Held in Late-May each year. With 4 distilleries situated on different Hebridean islands.
  https://hebrideanwhisky.com

# July

## Cantilena Festival

- Chamber Music performed by Cantilena's professional musicians and students of the Royal Conservatoire of Scotland. Held annually in July at various venues on Islay.
  www.cantilenafestival.co.uk

## HebCelt Festival

- Four-day Traditional Celtic Music Festival usually held in July at various venues on the Hebrides.
  www.hebceltfest.com

### Tarbert Seafood Festival

- Held Annually in the first full weekend of July. www.tarbertlochfyne.com

# August

## Mull of Kintyre Music Festival

- Held annually every August in Campbeltown. www.explorecampbeltown.com

# September

## Tarbert Music Festival

- Featuring contemporary and traditional Scottish Music. Held Annually in mid-September. www.tarbertlochfyne.com

# October

## Royal National Mòd

- The Mòd is a celebration of [Scottish] Gaelic language and culture, with a different host city/town each year.
  www.ancomunn.co.uk

# December

## Hogmanay (New Year) Parties to consider

- The whole of Scotland celebrates the turning of the year over a 3-day period with huge parties or just dropping in on the neighbors. Most of the cities or towns will have something going on, here are a few of the larger towns that hold a celebration; Aberdeen, Falkirk, Lerwick, Musselburgh, Stirling, Stonehaven, Stromness.
  www.scotland.org/events/hogmanay/hogmanay-events

# Chapter 6

## Additional Information

### Driving an electric car?

I have mentioned which towns/cities have charging stations, but for a more comprehensive list/map see the following website.
https://chargeplacescotland.org/live-map

### Midges

As you would expect from the country that brought you "Nessie" the loch Ness monster, the Highland midge" has taken on an almost mythical status.  I have heard it described as being about the size of a period (full stop) at the end of a sentence, with the teeth of an alligator.
First things first, midges do not transmit diseases to humans, about the only thing transmitted will be the tall tales that you'll tell when you return home.  The "midgie" as it is known in Scotland is so small that if you are walking, the wind of your passing will stop it from landing on you.  If there is a slight breeze you are safe, in fact about the only time that you are likely to get bitten is while asleep (mainly if you are camping).
Almost every hotel in the highlands of Scotland will have a warning about keeping your windows closed, because of the midges.

After all that, the bite doesn't hurt it just itches. You can use any insect repellant that would work for mosquitoes to keep them at bay or the old traditional method is to crush bog myrtle leaves in your palms and rub it on the exposed areas of skin. Which I have done to good effect in the past.

Growing up in Scotland and travelling back there on many trips, the midges was pretty much a non-event, until the summer of 2016. We stopped at Kinloch Lodge on the Isle of Skye for the night, and I noticed midges (lots of them) coming in through the windows, they were so small the seals couldn't stop them. I went to the local village to a grocery store for repellant, but they had none (obviously the locals are tougher than me). On the way back to the hotel I saw Bog Myrtle growing and stopped to pick some.

Back in the room I crushed some leaves on a few small branches, which I intertwined on the portable fan and pointed it at our bed, we were not bitten that night.

Our friend David was in another part of the hotel, so I called him and told him what to do, he declined. He got badly bitten that night.

The next night was spent at the Inverbeg Hotel in the village of Luss on Loch Lomond, that night we had no problems. The following morning when we were trying to get our bags into the car, we were attacked by more midges, than I have ever seen. They may be small, but us three adults jumped in the car and drove away as fast as we could. Un-fortunately they had come with us and we had to drive along with the windows open to try and get rid of them.

Next time we go to Scotland I am taking some mosquito repellant, better safe than sorry.

They are not a problem during the winter in Scotland as the first frost usually kills them off.

## Nationwide bus companies

- Citylink
  www.citylink.co.uk

- Megabus
  https://uk.megabus.com

- National
  www.nationalexpress.com

- Stagecoach
  www.stagecoachbus.com

## ScotRail

- National Rail Enquiries
  www.scotrail.co.uk

## Passports

Take a photo of your passport with your phone that way
if you lose your Passport, you have your Passport
information on your phone.
If you are worried about keeping that on your phone you
could e-mail it (and your itinerary) to someone you trust
back home.  That way if you lose your passport, they will
have the information available to help you get back
home.

# Bibliography

I have put links to all the places listed in this book and would like to thank them all for the information I have gathered in here. The information in this book is a snapshot of each of the places listed and for more in depth information, I suggest you go to the website of the place that you are interested in.
I would also like to thank the following sources;

## Affric Kintail Way

www.affrickintailway.com

## Along Dusty Roads

www.alongdustyroads.com

## Arran Coastal Way

www.coastalway.co.uk

## Atlas Obscura

www.atlasobscura.com

## Canmore

https://canmore.org.uk

## ChargePlace Scotland

https://chargeplacescotland.org

## CityLink Buses
www.citylink.co.uk

## Cowal way
www.cowalway.co.uk

## ebooks Visit Scotland
https://ebooks.visitscotland.com

## Encyclopedia Britannica
www.britannica.com

## Historic Environment Scotland
www.historicenvironment.scot

## Historic UK
www.historic-uk.com

## Kintyre Way
www.kintyreway.com

## Long Distance Walking Association
www.ldwa.org.uk

## Megabus Buses
https://uk.megabus.com

## National Buses
www.nationalexpress.com

## National Trust Scotland
www.nts.org.uk

## Scotrail
www.scotrail.co.uk

## Stagecoach Buses
www.stagecoachbus.com

## The West Highland Way
www.westhighlandway.org

## Trip Advisor
www.tripadvisor.com

## Virtual Hebrides
www.virtualheb.co.uk

## Visit Britain
www.visitbritain.com

## Visit Outer Hebrides
www.visitouterhebrides.co.uk

## Visit Scotland
www.visitscotland.com

## Watch me See
https://watchmesee.com

## Wikivoyage
https://en.wikivoyage.org

## Wikipedia
www.wikipedia.org

# Biography

Paul Bissett was born in Edinburgh, Scotland and raised in the village of Blackness on the river Forth. At the age of seventeen he embarked upon a twenty-three-year career in the British Royal Navy, which took him all over the world. He has lived and worked in seven different countries.

He has, at various times been; a mountain guide; made and installed kilns in Australia; an instructor in Saudi Arabia; a Documentation Manager for a software company in Taiwan; and in the USA been a salesman for Sears, a firefighter, an Emergency Medical Technician (EMT), a jewelry store manager, senior case manager for the National Expert Witness Network based in Paradise, California and recently became an Independent Contractor for International Network in Advance-Gaming Inc., covering California.

Outside of work, he conducts Celtic and Scottish weddings. Hosts whiskey tastings, in California, Nevada and Oregon. For fun, he researches whisky bars, writes/edits a whisky newsletter that go out to readers in ten different countries. He also gives talks on all things Scottish and has been the Master of Ceremonies at many events all over the world, including the Las Vegas Celtic Games (twice).

He currently lives in Yuba City, California, with his wife Tracey and their three dogs, Heather, Hamish and Luna.

Also, by Paul Bissett;

# Children's books

**Winter's Bite** – (Book one in the series). A modern-day adventure set in Scotland based on Scottish mythology.

**Destiny's Bite** - (Book two in the series). A modern-day adventure set in Scotland based on Scottish mythology.

# Cigars

**Cigar Traveler** - A guide to Cigar lounges in USA.

# Travel Books

**From Milngavie to Midges** - Hiking the "West Highland Way, Scotland."

**Hiking with Nessie** - Hiking the "Great Glen Way, Scotland."

**Touring Central Scotland** – Edinburgh, Falkirk, Glasgow, Stirling etc.

**Touring Orkney, Shetland & the North Western Highlands** - Including the North Coast 500.

**Touring Scotland** - A guide to help you plan the trip of a lifetime.

**Touring Southern Scotland** - Galashiels, Selkirk, Melrose, Hawick, Kelso, Jedburgh & Ayr, Dumfries etc.

**Touring the North East of Scotland** - Aberdeen, Dundee, Perth, Royal Deeside, Speyside etc.

**Touring the West Coast and the Western Isles of Scotland** – Campbeltown, Fort William, Islay, Jura, Mallaig, Oban & Skye.

# Whisk(e)y Books

**A Whisky Might Not Fix Things, But It's Worth A Shot!** - Whisk(e)y related: Anecdotes, Humor, Jokes, Memes, Quotes, Toasts & Trivia.

**Scotland's Single Malt Whisky Distilleries.** Where they are, when they were founded, how to pronounce their names (and what those names mean). I have also included a review of a whisky from each distillery.

**Whisky Timeline** - Whisk(e)y distilleries around the world and when they were founded.

**Whiskey Traveler** - A guide to Whisk(e)y bars around the world.

**Whiskey Traveler America** – Whiskey bars in every state.

**Whiskey Traveler Great Britain** - Whisky bars in England, Northern Ireland, Republic of Ireland, Scotland & Wales.


All books are available at www.amazon.com

My email is; paulwbissett@outlook.com

My website is; www.scot-talks.com